Uneasy Lives

Understanding

ANXIETY

DISORDERS

Senior Consulting Editor Carol C. Nadelson, M.D.
Consulting Editor Claire E. Reinburg

Uneasy Lives
Understanding
ANXIETY
DISORDERS

Linda Bayer, Ph.D.

CHELSEA HOUSE PUBLISHERS
Philadelphia

The author dedicates this book to Karena Bedient, whose courage, insight, and strength of character are an inspiration to all who know her. With wit, charm, and perseverance, she weathered threatening storms. In passion, intellect, and spirit, she lives intensely. A model mother, Karena demonstrates indomitable beauty in the face of disability.

The ENCYCLOPEDIA OF PSYCHOLOGICAL DISORDERS provides up-to-date information on the history of, causes and effects of, and treatment and therapies for problems affecting the human mind. The titles in this series are not intended to take the place of the professional advice of a psychiatrist or mental health care professional.

Chelsea House Publishers
Editor in Chief: Stephen Reginald
Production Manager: Pamela Loos
Art Director: Sara Davis
Director of Photography: Judy L. Hasday
Managing Editor: James D. Gallagher

Staff for UNEASY LIVES: UNDERSTANDING ANXIETY DISORDERS
Prepared by P. M. Gordon Associates, Philadelphia
Picture Researcher: Gillian Speeth, Picture This
Associate Art Director: Takeshi Takahashi
Cover Designer: Emiliano Begnardi

The Chelsea House World Wide Web address is
http://www.chelseahouse.com

First Printing

9 8 7 6 5 4 3 2

Library of Congress Cataloging-in-Publication Data

Applied for
ISBN 0-7910-5316-4

CONTENTS

PSYCHOLOGICAL DISORDERS AND THEIR EFFECT

CAROL C. NADELSON, M.D.
PRESIDENT AND CHIEF EXECUTIVE OFFICER,
The American Psychiatric Press

There are a wide range of problems that are considered psychological disorders, including mental and emotional disorders, problems related to alcohol and drug abuse, and some diseases that cause both emotional and physical symptoms. Psychological disorders often begin in early childhood, but during adolescence we see a sharp increase in the number of people affected by these disorders. It has been estimated that about 20 percent of the U.S. population will have some form of mental disorder sometime during their lifetime. Some psychological disorders appear following severe stress or trauma. Others appear to occur more often in some families and may have a genetic or inherited component. Still other disorders do not seem to be connected to any cause we can yet identify. There has been a great deal of attention paid to learning about the causes and treatments of these disorders, and exciting new research has taught us a great deal in the past few decades.

The fact that many new and successful treatments are available makes it especially important that we reject old prejudices and outmoded ideas that consider mental disorders to be untreatable. If psychological problems are identified early, it is possible to prevent serious consequences. We should not keep these problems hidden or feel shame that we or a member of our family has a mental disorder. Some people believe that something they said or did caused a mental disorder. Some people think that these disorders are "only in your head" so that you could "snap out of it" if you made the effort. This type of thinking implies that a treatment is a matter of willpower or motivation. It is a terrible burden for someone who is suffering to be blamed for his or her misery, and often people with psychological disorders are not treated compassionately. We hope that the information in this book will teach you about various mental illnesses.

The problems covered in the volumes in the ENCYCLOPEDIA OF PSYCHOLOGICAL DISORDERS were selected because they are of particular importance to young adults, because they affect them directly or because they affect family and friends. There are individual volumes on reading disorders, attention deficit and disruptive behavior disorders, and dementia—all of these are related to our abilities to learn and integrate information from the world around us. There are books on drug abuse that provide useful information about the effects of these drugs and treatments that are available for those individuals who have drug problems. Some of the books concentrate on one of the most common mental disorders, depression. Others deal with eating disorders, which are dangerous illnesses that affect a large number of young adults, especially women.

Most of the public attention paid to these disorders arises from a particular incident involving a celebrity that awakens us to our own vulnerability to psychological problems. These incidents of celebrities or public figures revealing their own psychological problems can also enable us to think about what we can do to prevent and treat these types of problems.

Although anxiety is a natural reaction to life's stresses and dangers, it can escalate into a serious condition known as anxiety disorder.

ANXIETY DISORDERS: AN OVERVIEW

Anxiety is a natural human response to tense or hazardous situations. It is vital, in fact, for survival. A person with too little anxiety might fail to take sufficient precautions in a dangerous environment. On a daily basis, an appropriate amount of anxiety helps spur us on—to finish an assignment on time, for instance, or to prepare for a big test or presentation. When anxiety gets out of control, however—when it dominates a person's life—it can become a crippling affliction.

Anxiety disorders are the most common type of mental illness. Often they include *panic attacks*, in which the person is overcome by fear, trembling, and other disturbing sensations. Sometimes they relate to a specific object: a person might have an uncontrollable fear of insects, for example. They may involve ritualized, repetitive behaviors that the person feels compelled to perform, such as repeated hand washing. Or they may include paralyzing flashbacks to a traumatic event experienced by the person earlier in life.

The typical causes of anxiety disorders seem to include both biology and environment. Researchers have begun to identify the biological mechanisms at work, and various studies show that an individual's susceptibility to anxiety disorders can be inherited from his or her parents. Yet each person's own experiences—the stresses and traumas of an individual's environment—also play an important role in triggering an anxiety problem.

This volume in the ENCYCLOPEDIA OF PSYCHOLOGICAL DISORDERS describes the various types of anxiety disorders, their symptoms, their possible causes, and their prevalence. Several case studies help reduce the mystery that typically surrounds these conditions. For each type of disorder, the book also explores current treatment options, including effective methods of psychotherapy and the use of medications.

The human ability to think about the future enables us to become fearful of what lies ahead. In some people, this basic survival mechanism veers out of control and develops into an anxiety disorder.

1

WHAT ARE ANXIETY DISORDERS?

Everybody feels anxious at times. A student feels anxiety before a big exam. An athlete becomes anxious before a big game. Couples experience anxiety on their first date. A top executive feels anxious when facing the responsibility of giving a major speech or undertaking an important negotiation.

In fact, anxiety—feeling uneasy or fearful about something in the future— is so common to modern humans that our time has been called an "age of anxiety." Psychologist Rollo May's book *The Meaning of Anxiety* calls anxiety "the nameless and formless uneasiness" that has "dogged the footsteps" of modern humans.

Whenever we feel anxious, the sensation is nearly always unpleasant. We would rather not be anxious. Why, then, do we succumb to the feeling so frequently?

THE USES OF ANXIETY

Feelings of anxiety seem to be natural, built-in responses to our environment. Basic fear, of course, is the emotional warning signal that alerts us to danger and motivates us to deal with an immediate threat. Anxiety is essentially fear that's projected into the future.

Because humans have the intelligence to imagine and ponder the future, we can also become fearful about it. And to the extent that our anxiety is well-founded, it serves as a survival mechanism. Sigmund Freud, often called the father of psychoanalysis, recognized "anxious readiness" as a feature of self-preservation that protects us from being caught off guard by sudden threats.

If we're anxious about an upcoming challenge, we are more likely to plan for it. Moreover, when we enter the challenging situation, our anxiety heightens our alertness, keeping our adrenaline flowing and our blood pumping rapidly. Thus prepared, we increase our chance of success.

Feeling anxious about an upcoming event can push us to prepare for it. These athletes—who are experiencing the uneasy feeling that typically precedes a major competition—benefit from the increased alertness, adrenaline, and blood flow that accompany the reaction.

Some thinkers have argued that, on a more intellectual level, anxiety can lead us to gain deep insights into reality. "Learning to know anxiety," wrote philosopher Søren Kierkegaard in *The Concept of Dread,* "is an adventure. . . . [The person] who has learned rightly to be anxious has learned the most important thing."

WHEN ANXIETY BECOMES A PROBLEM

Like most good things, too much anxiety can be problematic. Instead of helping to protect a person, it can become a hindrance or even a danger in itself.

Naturalist Charles Darwin's *The Expression of the Emotions in Man and Animals,* published in 1872, describes what happens to many animals when their lives are threatened:

Too much anxiety becomes a hindrance rather than a help. This 16-year-old fights a panic attack triggered by the task of selecting a song to perform in front of her music class.

TV sports personality and former Oakland Raiders head coach John Madden is known for his resolute refusal to travel by plane. Here he is seen riding in his custom-made bus, donated by Greyhound for Madden's frequent cross-country trips to broadcast games.

> With all or almost all animals, even with birds, terror causes the body to tremble. The skin becomes pale, sweat breaks out, and hair bristles. . . . The breathing is hurried. The heart beats quickly, wildly, and violently; but whether it pumps the blood more efficiently through the body may be doubted, for the surface seems bloodless and the strength of the muscles soon fails. . . .
>
> The mental faculties are much disturbed. Utter prostration soon follows, and even fainting. A terrified canary-bird has been seen not only to tremble and to turn white about the base of the bill, but to faint; and I once caught a robin in a room, which fainted so completely that for a time I thought it was dead.

As Darwin recognized, this type of reaction hardly seems useful from the standpoint of survival. The alarm system appears to be set too high for maximum efficiency. In the same way, people in certain situations become too panicked to help themselves.

With humans, this crippling panic can extend into the future as well, even in circumstances that they recognize as unworthy of such fear. American sportscaster and former football coach John Madden is a case in point. A 6-foot-4-inch, 260-pound man, Madden was terrified to fly on airplanes. Required to travel cross-country to coach, and later to broadcast games, he often spent days aboard a train rather than fly in a plane. Madden was aware that statistics prove that air travel is safer than ground transportation, but he could do nothing to stop his irrational fear. In fact, his panic attacks were not limited to flying; whenever he entered a small enclosure, such as an airplane cabin, he was overcome by terror.

In some respects, panic attacks resemble allergic reactions. Just as a person with allergies may respond with fear at being exposed to pollen, dog hair, perfume, or other usually harmless substances, a person with extreme anxiety may react to an ordinary situation as if it were dangerous. In such cases the problem is not the situation itself but the person's overwhelming reaction to it.

Even when anxiety doesn't result in a panic attack, it can disrupt a person's life. It can turn potentially enjoyable situations into uncomfortable, stressful experiences; it can put an individual's relationships with other people at risk; and, at the very least, it can generate a substantial waste of energy.

TYPES OF ANXIETY DISORDERS

If a person's anxiety is frequent and severe, he or she may be suffering from an *anxiety disorder.* The fourth edition of the American Psychiatric Association's *Diagnostic and Statistical Manual of Mental Disorders* (known as *DSM-IV*) describes several major types of anxiety disorders:

- *Panic disorder:* recurrent, unexpected panic attacks (see the sidebar "What Is a Panic Attack?" on p. 17) accompanied by concern about the attacks or by other behavioral changes

- *Phobias:* persistent, irrational fear of an object, activity, or situation

- *Posttraumatic stress disorder:* fear, horror, and other symptoms resulting from a traumatic experience, such as child abuse or war

- *Acute stress disorder:* a condition similar to, but not as long lasting as, posttraumatic stress disorder

- *Obsessive-compulsive disorder:* time-consuming, distressful obsessions (persistent thoughts or ideas) or compulsions (repetitive behaviors that the person feels driven to perform)

- *Generalized anxiety disorder:* excessive worry, difficult to control, that occurs commonly over a period of at least six months

- *Anxiety disorder resulting from a general medical condition:* excessive anxiety that is diagnosed as a direct physiological consequence of another medical condition

- *Substance-induced anxiety disorder:* prominent anxiety symptoms directly related to a person's exposure to a particular substance, such as a drug or a poison

Each of these anxiety disorders is discussed further in the following chapters.

According to the National Institute of Mental Health, anxiety disorders are the most common mental health problem in the United States—far surpassing depression, which many people believe to be the number one psychological illness. More than 19 million Americans suffer from an anxiety disorder each year, and the cost of treating these conditions amounts to about one-third of the country's mental health costs. In fact, alcohol and drug abuse—a major concern for many Americans—can often be attributed to an attempt at self-medication by people who are suffering from anxiety.

In addition to affecting mental health, anxiety disorders can cause physical health problems. According to two different studies conducted by W. Coryell and other researchers, both inpatients and outpatients who have been diagnosed with anxiety disorders, particularly those involving panic attacks, have a higher mortality rate than that of the rest of the population. Cardiovascular disease (among males) and suicide account for many of these additional deaths.

WHAT IS A PANIC ATTACK?

I n the *DSM-IV*'s classification of anxiety disorders, a panic attack does not by itself constitute a disorder. Rather, a panic attack can occur as a result of any of the anxiety disorders described in this book. Panic disorder, phobias, and posttraumatic stress disorder, for example, can each produce a panic attack at one time or another.

What does a panic attack involve? It is characterized by intense fear or discomfort that begins suddenly–"out of the clear blue," as one sufferer put it. The attack builds rapidly, usually peaking within 10 minutes. The person often has a sense of impending danger or doom and an urge to escape. For the episode to be classified as a full-fledged panic attack, it must also include at least four of the following symptoms:

- Chest pain or discomfort

- Chills or hot flashes

- Choking feeling

- Derealization (a feeling of unreality) or depersonalization (the feeling of being detached from oneself)

- Dizziness, unsteadiness, light-headedness, or faintness

- Fear of dying

- Fear of losing control or going crazy

- Heart palpitations, pounding heart, or accelerated heart rate

- Nausea or abdominal distress

- Paresthesia (a numbness or tingling sensation)

- Shortness of breath or the sensation of being smothered

- Sweating

- Trembling or shaking

Psychotherapy and medication are both effective methods of treating anxiety disorders. This 14-year-old takes antidepressants to control her obsessive-compulsive disorder.

Fortunately, there are successful methods of treating anxiety disorders. Psychotherapy ("talk" therapy) and such medications as *antidepressants* have both proven effective; these treatments are described in subsequent chapters. Resources for finding help are listed in Appendix: For More Information.

For many people with panic disorder, a stressful life event precedes the first attack. Even seemingly positive life changes—such as a promotion or an increase in job responsibility—can act as stressors.

PANIC DISORDER

R ay was a 30-year-old man who had a good corporate job. He had just received an important promotion. Although Ray's father had recently died, which left Ray without a key source of emotional support, he had the comfort of a girlfriend who was caring and sympathetic. Bright and conscientious, Ray seemed to be quite successful.

One night, however, Ray was suddenly overwhelmed by a feeling of dread. In Michael Zal's book *Panic Disorder: The Great Pretender*, he describes Ray's condition:

> He wanted to scream. He wanted to run and get help. He wanted to hide. But he could not focus his mind to cope with the onslaught of terror. His heart raced and seemed to want to jump out of his chest. He was short of breath and felt as if he was smothering.
>
> Ray tried to walk but was weak and unsteady on his feet. When he finally got to the bed, he lay there huddled and trembling, sure that he was dying or having a heart attack. He would later learn that he had had his first panic attack.

At first Ray ignored the incident, but 10 days later he had his second attack, closely resembling the first. This time Ray went to the hospital emergency room, where he was evaluated and assured that he had no detectable medical problem.

During the next year, however, Ray continued to have episodic attacks of overwhelming anxiety. Although multiple trips to the hospital produced no specific diagnosis, Ray felt sure he was suffering from a cardiac problem. Eventually, after giving Ray repeated stress tests, cardiac evaluations, and echocardiograms, his doctors diagnosed mitral prolapse (a relatively benign problem involving a heart valve) and assured Ray that he had no serious heart condition.

Ray's helpless, hopeless mood during attacks was in stark contrast to his normal independent, productive personality. In time Ray's girlfriend lost patience with the problem; she wanted Ray to "grow up." Finally, a family physician suggested that there might be some emotional basis for the attacks. After suffering with the condition for more than a year, Ray was diagnosed with a panic disorder.

■   ■   ■

As Ray's case demonstrates, panic disorder is characterized by panic attacks that occur repeatedly and at unexpected moments. There usually appears to be no specific trigger; the onset of an attack can occur even during sleep. One of the first signs of an attack is often *hyperventilation,* an abnormally fast or deep breathing pattern that can cause dizziness.

The attacks usually cause the sufferer to worry about his or her health—often leaving the person convinced, like Ray, that some dire physical condition is responsible for the problem. Yet, when doctors investigate, they find no direct link to a physical disorder.

Panic disorder can be extremely disabling. The fear of future attacks typically presents more of a problem than an attack itself. Individuals with panic disorder may also become afraid of neutral aspects of an attack, such as the time of day that it occurred, the clothes they were wearing during the attack, or the place where it occurred. Fearing future attacks, sufferers often avoid work or social situations. They may resist going anywhere without a spouse or friend to assist them in case panic strikes.

In as many as half the cases of panic disorder, the tendency to avoid the outside world becomes so severe that it develops into *agoraphobia.* Derived from ancient Greek, the word *agoraphobia* literally means "fear of the market place." Today the term is used to describe a general fear of open spaces, the outdoors, or overcrowded areas. Afraid that an attack would embarrass them or that they would be unable to get help in such environments, people with the agoraphobic form of panic disorder regularly avoid these places. (Chapter 4 provides a detailed discussion of agoraphobia.)

WHO GETS PANIC DISORDER?

According to statistics from the National Institute of Mental Health (NIMH), between 3 and 6 million Americans suffer from panic disorder. The *DSM-IV* estimates that between 1.5 percent and 3.5 percent of the world's people will have panic disorder at one time or another during their lives. The disease occurs twice as often among women as among men. Although it can occur at any age, it most often begins in young adulthood. The average patient develops panic disorder at about 20 years of age.

People who suffer from panic attacks can become substance abusers. In an attempt to tranquilize themselves, many sufferers turn to using alcohol or drugs. Feelings of hopelessness and self-blame also frequently accompany panic disorder. According to the NIMH, about one-fifth of those who suffer from panic disorder attempt suicide.

Many researchers have attempted to identify the causes of panic disorder. To date, no single culprit has been found. Rather, various elements seem to work together to bring on the attacks.

EMOTIONAL AND ENVIRONMENTAL FACTORS

In the *Handbook of Anxiety*, M. Roth, R. Noyes, and G. Burrows sum up many of the emotional factors associated with panic disorder. People with low self-esteem are more likely than the remainder of the general population to develop panic disorders, as are people who tend either to avoid or to become unusually dependent on others. According to the *DSM-IV*, as many as 65 percent of people with panic disorder also experience serious depression; in one-third of those cases, the onset of depression occurs first. It appears, then, that certain preexisting psychological problems may lead to panic disorder.

A person's immediate situation may also play a role. Some studies suggest that, in the majority of cases, people with panic disorder have experienced an unusually stressful life event shortly before the first attack. Stressful events include a major change in home or family life, a divorce or breakup of a relationship, and the loss or birth of a child (often the birth of a second child). A typical stressful event at work is an increase in responsibility, possibly because of a promotion or an increased workload. Other common stressors are surgery, illness, auto accidents, and serious injuries. Interestingly, many studies indicate that the body may interpret change as stressful regardless of whether the new circumstance is bad or good. For instance, marriage and new employment can produce stress even though both events may represent improvement in a person's life.

The role of stress in causing panic disorder may explain why young adults are particularly prone to this problem. When in their early twenties, people are typically faced with increased responsibility; a variety of new issues associated with independence, career, and relationship choices; and separation from their parents. Stress during such transitional periods is usually high.

HEREDITARY AND BIOLOGICAL FACTORS

A number of research findings indicate that a predisposition to developing panic disorder is hereditary—that is, it runs in families. Close relatives of people with panic disorder are much more likely to develop the disease than is the average person. Similarly, studies of twins show that if one identical twin has the disorder, the other twin is very likely to develop it as well. No such correlation has been found for fraternal twins, who are not genetically identical.

As Mary Lynn Hendrix notes in her book *Understanding Panic Disorder*, these studies suggest that "some genetic factor, in combination with environment, may be responsible for vulnerability to this condition." Researchers are currently attempting to isolate the particular gene or combination of genes that may be involved.

Other research on the origins of panic disorder has focused on the deficiency or excess of certain chemicals in the body. Physicians have observed that the consumption of large amounts of caffeine—for example, five or more cups of coffee a day—can bring on a panic attack in a person who is predisposed to the condition. In the same way, it is possible to set off an attack by intravenous administration of sodium lactate, a chemical that tends to accumulate naturally in the muscles during strenuous exercise. If these substances can trigger panic, might there be a similar chemical working in the body that is responsible for the onset of panic attacks?

Researchers such as J. P. Boulenger and D. S. Charney have shown that panic attacks may be caused by a variety of substances, including carbon dioxide, yohimbine (a poisonous substance derived from the bark of a tree), and marijuana. Again, these results all point to a chemical source for the problem.

Some researchers have looked at mechanisms involving the hormones adrenaline and noradrenaline, which are normally released by the body during stress. At times of extreme danger, the release of these hormones helps create the *fight-or-flight response* typical in both human

Research points to the existence of a genetic predisposition to panic disorder. When one identical twin suffers from the condition, for example, the chances greatly increase that the other twin will develop the disorder.

beings and animals. In this response, the heart rate accelerates and the rate of respiration increases, which ensures that additional amounts of blood and oxygen reach the brain and muscles. The individual can thus react more quickly, run faster, or attack with greater force. Some researchers suggest that panic disorder occurs when a defective bio-chemical trigger releases adrenaline and noradrenaline, setting off a fight-or-flight response in the absence of any real danger—like a faulty smoke alarm that goes off when there is no fire.

Some researchers have studied panic disorder by using positron emission tomography (PET scans), a technique that provides pictures of the physiological changes taking place in the brain. Such studies show

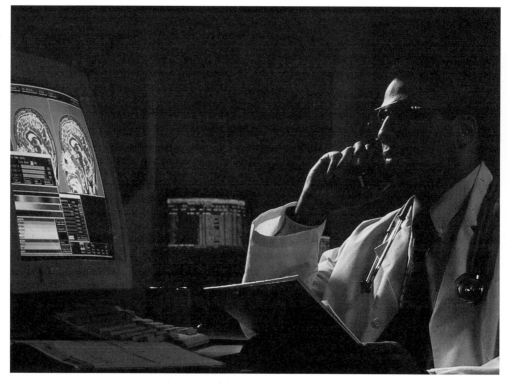

Some studies indicate that biochemical mechanisms are involved in panic disorder. PET scans (positron emission tomography), such as the one shown here, supply images of physiological changes in the brain.

that patients suffering from panic attacks have abnormally high rates of oxygen metabolism, blood flow, and blood volume in certain areas of the brain. This increased brain cell activity may help trigger attacks.

Another theory involves the regulation of antianxiety substances in the body. These substances normally act on certain nerve receptors to reduce anxiety. Researchers speculate that this mechanism may fail to function during panic attacks.

Whatever the biochemical mechanism involved—and there may be more than one—it probably works in concert with the individual's life experiences to cause a breakdown of the body's normal way of coping with the environment. As explained in the NIMH booklet *Panic Disorder Treatment and Referral*, "Some researchers theorize that the disturbance in coping mechanisms is a product of repeated life stresses in predisposed individuals, leading eventually to panic disorder." Put simply, the causation pattern for panic disorder may look like this:

- First, a person is predisposed to panic disorder because he or she has inherited certain genes.

- The person undergoes repeated, normal life stresses that, because of his or her genetic predisposition, cause changes in the body's chemistry.

- Because of these changes in biochemistry, the person's internal alarm system becomes faulty or oversensitive, making the individual more likely to suffer panic attacks.

- Finally, when the attacks become frequent enough to cause a serious problem, the individual is considered to have panic disorder.

TREATMENT

In some cases of panic disorder, the symptoms eventually cease on their own. Or the symptoms may go into remission for many years, only to reappear at a time of severe stress. In other cases, although the panic attacks have ceased, the patient remains anxious about the possibility of recurrence. Some individuals have only occasional mild attacks.

Unfortunately, in many cases if the condition is left untreated, people with panic disorder will become agoraphobic and, as a result, housebound. Some individuals experience such incapacitation and dysfunction that their anxiety over the original panic attacks is replaced by concern about the complications caused by the attacks. Clearly, panic disorder is not a condition that a person should try to endure alone. Medical treatment is important—and it has a high rate of success. The NIMH estimates that 70 to 90 percent of patients with panic disorder can be significantly helped by treatment.

As with other psychological disorders, treatment falls into two basic types: psychotherapy and the use of medication. Often the two methods are combined.

PSYCHOTHERAPY

A form of psychotherapy frequently effective for panic disorder is *cognitive-behavioral therapy*. This is a combination of the *cognitive approach*, in which the therapist focuses on a person's patterns of thinking, and the *behavioral approach*, in which the therapist tries to identify and change problematic behaviors.

In treating panic disorder, cognitive-behavioral therapists try to break the cycle in which a small anxious sensation triggers a larger worry, which in turn sets off a greater anxiety, and so on, until a full-fledged panic attack is under way. The therapist helps the patient identify the earliest thoughts, feelings, and sensations that occur in a typical attack. The individual can then learn to recognize these as signs of an imminent attack as soon as they appear. And with the therapist's help, the patient can begin to change his or her reaction to them—by deliberately thinking different thoughts or by engaging in systematic relaxation techniques, for example.

One early symptom of an oncoming attack, for instance, might be hyperventilation. This extremely rapid breathing may in turn make the patient think, "Oh no, I'm going to die." In this case the therapist can help the individual learn to control the breathing and change his or her thought pattern as follows: To stop hyperventilating, the patient can use exercises that resemble the controlled breathing taught in Lamaze childbirth classes and practiced during meditation by Buddhist monks. Simultaneously, the patient can deliberately replace negative thoughts with such positive affirmations as "This is just another episode of hyperventilation, and I know how to keep it under control."

At some point the therapy may involve deliberately exposing the patient to a situation that would normally trigger a panic attack. If the patient has been avoiding crowded areas, for instance, the therapist may take the patient to a shopping center to help him or her practice handling the onset of panic symptoms. This "exposure" technique is, of course, implemented with care, allowing the patient to make one small advance at a time without serious setbacks.

Typically, cognitive-behavioral therapy for panic disorder lasts at least 8 to 12 weeks, with the patient seeing the therapist from one to three hours per week. Between sessions with the therapist, patients practice the techniques on their own. They may also join therapy groups of people with similar problems.

Psychodynamic therapy, a deeper-probing and longer-lasting type of psychotherapy, has also been used with patients suffering from panic disorder. In this treatment the therapist often focuses on the patient's past, attempting to uncover emotional problems that may be the root of the stress leading to the attacks. This method is especially helpful if, in addition to panic disorder, the patient has other psychological problems. Psychodynamic therapy by itself, however, is not very effective at relieving the symptoms of panic disorder. Cognitive-behavioral therapy is usually required as well.

USE OF MEDICATION

Two general types of prescription medication have been effective in reducing or even preventing panic attacks: antidepressants and *benzodiazepines*).

The first medications to prove useful for panic disorder came from a group of antidepressants called "tricyclics." Today the tricyclic most commonly prescribed is imipramine (marketed under the brand name Tofranil). Monoamine oxidase (MAO) inhibitors have also been used with success; among these, the most common is phenelzine (Nardil). A newer class of antidepressants, selective serotonin reuptake inhibitors (SSRIs) such as fluoxetine (Prozac) and sertraline (Zoloft), has also proved effective in certain cases. The course of treatment with any of the antidepressants generally lasts from 6 to 12 months. The dosage begins at a low level and is gradually increased until it provides effective results.

Benzodiazepines are a powerful type of antianxiety medication, sometimes referred to as "major tranquilizers." Among these, alprazolam (Xanax), clonazepam (Klonopin), and lorazepam (Ativan) have all been successfully prescribed for treating panic disorder. Because patients using benzodiazepines may experience withdrawal symptoms when use of the drug is discontinued, however, both the dosage and patient reaction must be closely monitored.

Many therapists advocate combining medication and psychotherapy, so that each form of treatment supports the other. While the medicine provides short-term relief of symptoms, the patient has the opportunity to develop cognitive and behavioral techniques to ward off attacks in the long term.

Fears concerning circumstances that signal danger have survival value. If they become excessive, however, they may be considered phobias. The woman on the bridge suffers from acrophobia, the fear of heights.

3

PHBIAS

Fear is a primordial response shared by humans and animals. As the previous chapters point out, fear helps prepare an individual to either escape from or confront a threat. Because fear causes the heart and the lungs to start working faster, the individual is better able to fight or to flee—whichever seems advisable under the circumstances. It is impossible to be inattentive or sluggish while frightened.

The similarity of the fear response in humans to that in many animals can be seen in our vestigial fright reactions—that is, those reactions that we continue to exhibit even though we no longer have any need for them. For example, when many mammals feel afraid, their fur stands on end, making them seem larger and more formidable to enemies. In the same way, when we are frightened or deeply moved emotionally, we get goose bumps, or the hair on our arms stands on end, even though humans are now so nearly hairless that no increase in size results.

Human fears resemble those of animals in other ways as well. Young children, like young animals, tend to be more fearful than adults. This makes good sense for purposes of survival, since the younger, smaller, and weaker are more vulnerable to predators. Similarly, humans and mammals in the animal world share other typical kinds of fears that have survival value, such as fear of heights, fire, large bodies of water, small enclosures where one might be trapped or crushed, and wide-open spaces where it is difficult to take cover.

What do these similarities tell us? They suggest that many of the most common fears exist in part because they helped our species survive in past ages. One reason that you and your dog may both fear lightning is that lightning can be a danger to both people and dogs.

But when a fear is out of control, going far beyond what is reasonable under the circumstances, it is no longer an aid for survival. In fact, it may become a liability. In this case it is called a phobia. Chapter 4 details the characteristics of one form of phobia, called agoraphobia. In this chapter we examine specific phobia and social phobia.

SPECIFIC PHOBIA

Specific phobia (formerly called simple phobia) refers to a persistent, excessive fear of a particular kind of object or situation, such as fear of snakes or insects or of being in storms, on airplanes, on bridges, or in small spaces. Whether the phobic stimulus is an object or a situation, exposure to it almost always provokes marked anxiety or even a full-blown panic attack.

For a phobic individual, merely thinking about the dreaded stimulus can precipitate symptoms such as heart palpitations, hyperventilation, profuse sweating, dizziness, nausea, abdominal cramps, cold or hot flashes, and abject terror. Adults who suffer from this kind of phobia recognize that their fears are out of proportion with the danger at hand, but this knowledge does little to reduce the sense of dread.

A diagnosis of specific phobia is not made unless the terror is unwarranted and impacts negatively on a person's life. For example, an individual with an unreasonable, intense fear of snakes is not labeled phobic if he or she lives in an area devoid of snakes and is rarely plagued by the thought of snakes. Similarly, a soldier who fears combat when most of his buddies have recently been killed in battle would not be called phobic, because his sense of fright is justified.

Sometimes phobias are confused with other disorders. For instance, a patient suffering from panic attacks who fears elevators and other enclosed places because a number of his or her attacks took place in elevators should be diagnosed with panic disorder rather than phobia. If, however, panic attacks occur *only* in elevators and small enclosures, the specific phobia called *claustrophobia* (abnormal fear of enclosed spaces) should be diagnosed. On the other hand, a patient whose fear of an elevator is based on a conviction that it has been sabotaged by aliens from Mars might be suffering from delusional disorder rather than a phobia. People with phobias have irrational reactions rather than unreasonable beliefs.

SUBTYPES OF SPECIFIC PHOBIA

The subtypes of specific phobia, listed in order of prevalence among adults (from most common to relatively rare), are as follows:

Specific phobias are categorized into five basic subtypes. Arachnophobia (the fear of spiders) is one example of the animal subtype.

1. *Situational type:* fear of a specific situation, such as being in a tunnel, on a bridge, in an elevator, in a plane, or in an enclosed place, as well as fear of driving and fear of public transportation

2. *Natural environment type:* fear set off by a place or some other aspect of the natural environment, such as a storm, a high place, or a body of water

3. *Blood-injection-injury type:* fear triggered by the sight of blood or of an injury or by receiving an injection or undergoing another kind of invasive medical procedure (according to the *DSM-IV*, about 75 percent of people with this disorder have a history of fainting when the phobia strikes, and many endanger their health by avoiding medical and dental care)

4. *Animal type:* fear of animals or insects—dogs, cats, snakes, spiders, and so on

5. *Other type:* a catchall category for phobias that do not fit in the first four types, such as a pathological avoidance of situations that might lead to illness (for instance, refusing to visit friends who have young children because children often have colds) or "space phobia" (in which the person does not want to be in large, open spaces because of fear of falling if there are no walls or other physical supports nearby)

It's natural from a survival standpoint for children—who are more vulnerable—to be more fearful than adults. For this reason, specific phobia is rarely diagnosed in anyone under age 18.

ONSET, PREVALENCE, AND ASSOCIATED FACTORS

For most kinds of specific phobia, the disorder typically begins in childhood. The situational type commonly begins either in childhood or in the mid-twenties. Fear of heights often develops during early adulthood, though it can begin in childhood as well.

Although phobias frequently begin during childhood, physicians are reluctant to diagnose the disorder at an early age. Irrational fear is common among children, and many grow out of it. Unless the problem persists for six months or more, a diagnosis of specific phobia is rarely made in children under 18 years of age.

It is important that therapists use the same discretion when diagnosing people from different cultures. In some cultures, fear of magic, spirits, the ghosts of ancestors, and other mystical beings may be an accepted part of a belief system. Followers are not considered phobic unless the fear is excessive within the context of the particular ethnic or religious group.

In general, having one type of phobia increases the chances of developing another phobia from the same subtype. For example, a person who is afraid of dogs may develop a fear of cats. Specific phobias may also occur in conjunction with other anxiety disorders.

People do not usually develop specific phobias unless they are predisposed to irrational fears. Given that vulnerability, however, a traumatic event, such as being bitten by a dog or trapped in a closet, can lead to a phobia connected with the trauma. Merely being exposed to information about specific dangers may have an impact as well; for instance, repeated warnings from parents and discussion in the media about car crashes may cause a vulnerable person to develop a phobia about riding in a motor vehicle.

As the discussion about the survival value of certain phobias suggests, objects and situations that have actually represented danger in the course of human life on earth are more likely to cause phobic reactions than are other items. Phobias involving water and fire are more common than fears of sunshine and flowers, presumably because of an innate sense that drowning and burning are genuine dangers.

The tendency to develop phobias runs in families, probably for both genetic and environmental reasons. That is, children can inherit a genetic susceptibility to develop a specific phobia, as they can for other anxiety disorders. But children can also observe fearful behavior on the

NAME THAT PHOBIA

Humans have found so many possible phobic stimuli in the world that a list of specific phobias would run on for pages. Some of the names that have been given to particular fears sound quaint or even comic. To the people who suffer from these conditions, however, they are far from a laughing matter. The following is a small sampling of names of specific phobias:

Acrophobia: fear of heights

Aerophobia: fear of flying

Ailurophobia: fear of cats

Algophobia: fear of pain

Amaxophobia: fear of riding in a car

Aquaphobia: fear of water

Arachnophobia: fear of spiders

Batrachophobia: fear of amphibians, such as frogs and toads

Bibliophobia: fear of books

Brontophobia: fear of thunder

Carcinophobia: fear of cancer

Claustrophobia: fear of closed or narrow spaces

Cynophobia: fear of dogs

Dendrophobia: fear of trees

Dromophobia: fear of crossing streets

Electrophobia: fear of electricity

Entomophobia: fear of insects

Gephyrophobia: fear of crossing bridges

Heliophobia: fear of the sun

Hematophobia: fear of blood

Herpetophobia: fear of reptiles

Hippophobia: fear of horses

Ichthyophobia: fear of fish

Leukophobia: fear of the color white

Melanophobia: fear of the color black

Microphobia: fear of small things

Musophobia: fear of mice

Mysophobia: fear of germs and dirt

Nyctophobia: fear of darkness or night

Ochlophobia: fear of crowds

Ophidiophobia: fear of snakes

Ornithophobia: fear of birds

Pyrophobia: fear of fire

Trichophobia: fear of hair

Triskaidekaphobia: fear of the number 13

Typanophobia: fear of injections

Xenophobia: fear of strangers, foreigners, or things that are strange or foreign

Zoophobia: fear of animals

part of phobic relatives, and this environmental influence may help set off a phobia of their own.

The *DSM-IV* estimates that about 10 to 11 percent of the people in the United States suffer from a specific phobia at one time or other during their lives. The disorder occurs more often among females than among males. This is particularly true for the situational, animal, and natural environment type phobias, for which females make up 75 to 90 percent of patients (except for fear of heights, in which females account for 55 to 70 percent). The reason for this gender difference is not yet known.

SOCIAL PHOBIA

Social phobia (formerly known as social anxiety disorder) is marked by a persistent fear of being in situations in which the individual might be embarrassed. If the phobic condition is severe enough, the situation may set off a panic attack. The situations in which the fear occurs may involve performance—for example, public speaking or musical performance—or they may be ordinary social occasions. A phobic person naturally tends to avoid these situations at all costs.

Though many people are nervous in social situations, people with social phobia find some or most public circumstances unbearable. They may fear certain specific situations: eating in restaurants, using public restrooms, drinking in front of other people, or talking to strangers. Or they may have a general fear that others will judge them harshly and conclude that they are weak, crazy, or stupid. These people are afraid to converse with others, assuming that they will make mistakes or appear inarticulate. They are usually very uncomfortable at parties or similar social events.

Some social phobics suffer from low self-esteem and have difficulty being assertive. They may exhibit poor social skills (not making eye contact, for example) or display signs of discomfort such as cold, clammy hands; shaky voice; and tremors.

Clearly, the symptoms of this disorder can interfere with the individual's daily life. People with social phobia may skip school, pass up job interviews, avoid jobs that require public speaking, and refrain from various forms of group participation. They may become underachievers whose academic and professional performances do not reflect their innate ability. Social phobics are also less likely to date, marry, and have satisfying friendships. Some, especially children, develop mutism (failure to speak).

Social phobia usually starts during the mid-teenage years. It may follow a childhood history of inhibition and shyness. The onset can be precipitated by a stressful, humiliating event, or the illness can develop gradually. The disorder can fade away during adulthood or persist throughout life. It may disappear for a time and then reappear during a moment of crisis: for example, the problem may diminish after marriage, only to return after the death of the person's spouse. Similarly, the phobia could reappear with a job promotion requiring that the person speak publicly.

Like specific phobias, social phobia may be diagnosed in several members of the same family. But estimates of the number of people with social phobia vary widely. Some studies report that no more than 3 percent of Americans have experienced social phobia; others put the figure as high as 13 percent. Because the various studies use different definitions of impairment and survey different groups of fears, it is difficult to arrive at precise figures. Similarly, though various surveys suggest that social phobia is more common among women than among men, the exact gender distribution remains unknown.

TREATMENT

Phobias that start at an early age and persist into adulthood do not often go into remission. According to the NIMH, only about 20 percent of such cases improve without treatment.

Like the treatment of panic disorder (described in chapter 2), the medical approach to phobias usually involves either cognitive-behavioral therapy, medication, or a combination of the two. Such treatment often has a high degree of success. For social phobia, for example, the NIMH estimates that improvement is evident in about 80 percent of the patients.

COGNITIVE-BEHAVIORAL THERAPY

When cognitive-behavioral therapy is used to treat phobia, a process known as *systematic desensitization* is often followed. This is an *exposure technique*, which involves deliberate and repeated exposure to the phobic stimulus (object or situation that sets off the phobic reaction) until, over time, the patient learns to become less sensitive.

Systematic desensitization is frequently used in cognitive-behavioral therapy for phobia. This young woman, who has been gradually exposed to her phobic stimulus, can now hold a snake without excessive fear.

For example, imagine a person who is deathly afraid of snakes. Early in the therapy, the patient may be asked to look at a picture of a snake. Gradually, the amount of time spent looking at the snake photographs is increased, until the visual image itself ceases to provoke dread.

Next the patient may be brought into the presence of a real snake—at a distance. Again, the time spent in a room with the snake is gradually increased, and little by little the patient moves closer to the animal. The subject is asked to pay attention to details: how the snake moves, how it sticks out its tongue, and how it eats. If the patient has a tendency to hyperventilate, this is controlled with breathing exercises. Each successful encounter sets the stage for the next step.

Eventually, the phobic person is encouraged to touch a harmless (nonpoisonous) snake. This pattern is repeated at intervals until the patient is no longer afraid of snakes or is much less anxious in their presence. Through systematic desensitization, the phobic individual can

"IT'S AN AWFUL FEELING"

To understand the severe difficulties that phobias can cause, imagine that you had to take an airplane trip even though you were deathly afraid of flying. The NIMH web page on anxiety disorders quotes the following account by a person with aerophobia:

> It's an awful feeling when that airplane door closes and I feel trapped. My heart pounds and I sweat bullets. If somebody starts talking to me, I get very stiff and preoccupied. When the airplane starts to ascend, it just reinforces that feeling that I can't get out. I picture myself losing control, freaking out, climbing the walls, but of course I never do. I'm not afraid of crashing or hitting turbulence. It's just that feeling of being trapped. Whenever I've thought about changing jobs, I've had to think, "Would I be under pressure to fly?" These days I only go places where I can drive or take a train. My friends always point out that I couldn't get off a train traveling at high speeds either, so why don't trains bother me? I just tell them it isn't a rational fear.

The mere thought of getting on an airplane can trigger a severe reaction in someone suffering from aerophobia (the fear of flying). Even sufferers who recognize their fear as irrational feel powerless to change it.

now remember encounters with the feared object that did not precipitate bad experiences.

Cognitive therapy is frequently used to reinforce the results of behavioral work. For example, a patient who is being desensitized to snakes may tend to think, "Things went well today, but that's just because I'm having a good day. If I see a picture of a snake tomorrow, I'll probably panic." With cognitive therapy, the phobic learns to set aside such self-defeating thought patterns in favor of more positive ones.

Group therapy versions of these approaches have the added advantage that patients can provide support for one another and offer each other models of success. Self-management programs have also been developed to help phobics continue their progress on their own. For example, a phobic who tends to be overly dependent on other people can use self-management to help build independence and self-esteem.

A "paradoxical" approach to cognitive-behavioral therapy calls for patients to immerse themselves in the feared environment and try to increase its negative effects. Phobics are instructed to focus on their physiological symptoms—heart palpitations, sweating, and dry mouth, for example—and to try to make these reactions worse. When the subject sees that no terrible result occurs—when the symptoms fail to lead to heart attack or death, for example—the patient's recovery may begin.

For individuals with social phobia, assertiveness training and classes in social skills have proven beneficial. As patients gradually increase their exposure to feared social situations, each small success helps reduce their fears that public appearances will lead to embarrassment or shame.

USE OF MEDICATION

As with treating panic disorder, the most useful types of medication for treating phobia have been antidepressants and benzodiazepines. People with a performance type of social phobia, such as musicians who suffer a paralyzing stage fright, have also been treated successfully with drugs called beta-blockers, which block the action of the hormone adrenaline at specific points in the body.

Many therapists have had the best results using medication in conjunction with behavioral and cognitive techniques. Addressing the body and mind together often produces better results than treating either alone.

Agoraphobia is an extreme fear of open spaces, the outdoors, and overcrowded places. These include such areas as city streets, shopping malls, and public transportation.

4

AGORAPHOBIA: THE FEAR OUT THERE

goraphobia is a severe anxiety about being in open spaces or public areas. Typically, the sufferer fears having panic symptoms in a place where escape might prove either difficult or embarrassing.

The cluster of symptoms lumped under the term *agoraphobia* indicates fear of public places and gatherings of various kinds: streets, shops, and crowds. Most agoraphobics experience fear of a number of public situations. They may, for example, dread any instance in which they have to stand in line or travel on a bus or train. Many people with this illness are afraid to leave their homes for any reason, while others are afraid to be alone in their houses.

Clearly, agoraphobia can keep patients from fulfilling many of their ordinary responsibilities: going to school or work, doing the grocery shopping, taking children to the doctor, and so on. Often, however, an agoraphobic who is accompanied by a trusted companion is able to tolerate places that he or she avoids when alone.

Agoraphobia, as noted in chapter 2, frequently accompanies panic disorder, which is characterized by a series of panic attacks. But agoraphobia can also exist without full-fledged panic attacks. For instance, a patient may fear that riding a bus will produce so much anxiety that he or she will become dizzy and fall. If this fear becomes so persistent and severe that the individual quits a job in order to avoid public transportation, the person may be diagnosed with agoraphobia even though he or she has not suffered a panic attack.

Some patients describe ploys that they use to help reduce their symptoms. They may venture out in the dark or in a storm, when crowded or open spaces are less visible. Or they may find that they are better able to endure public or open places if they are riding a bicycle instead of walking. Even gripping a suitcase may give them some sense of security.

Fearing that they will have a panic attack, agoraphobics typically avoid public situations. They often view areas that do not provide an easy means of escape—such as buses and trains—as particularly threatening.

■   ■   ■

The following autobiographical account was written by an American man who became agoraphobic at age 22, shortly after he was married. Although his story dates from 1890, when it was published in an article by S. W. Clevenger, the details on the manifestations of his illness differ little from those of today's patients. Each case has its own unique features, but the following heartbreaking account is fairly typical:

> I became morbidly sensitive about being brought into close contact with any large number of people. Finding myself in the midst of a large gathering would inspire a feeling of terror [which] . . . could be relieved in but one way—by getting away from the spot as soon

as possible. Acting on this impulse I have left churches, theatres, even funerals, simply because of an utter inability to control myself to stay. For 10 years I have not been to church, to the theatre, to political gatherings or to any form of popular meeting, except where I could remain in the background, with means of egress convenient. Even at my mother's funeral . . . I was utterly unable to bring myself to sit with the other members of the family in the front of the church. Not only has this unfortunate trait deprived me of an immense amount of pleasure and benefit, but it has also been a matter of considerable expense. More than once I have gotten off a crowded train halfway to the station for which I was bound, merely from my inability to stand the jostling and confusion incident to the occasion. Times more than I can recall I have gone into restaurants or dining rooms, ordered a meal and left it untouched, impelled by my desire to escape the crowd . . . [or] have bought tickets to theatres, concerts, fairs or whatnot, merely to give them away when the critical moment arrived and I realized the impossibility of my facing the throng with composure.

[A fear of open spaces] has been at times very pronounced. Many a time I have slunk in alleys instead of keeping on the broad streets, and often have walked long distances—perhaps a mile—to avoid crossing some pasture or open square, even when it was a matter of moment to me to save all the time possible. The dominating impulse is to always have something within reach to steady myself by in case of giddiness. The feeling is at times so strong that even when on a steamboat or a vessel, I cannot bear to look across any wide expanse of water, feeling almost impelled to jump in out of sheer desperation. . . . This malady . . . has throttled all ambition, and killed all personal pride, spoiled every pleasure.

ONSET AND COURSE OF AGORAPHOBIA

In some cases, agoraphobia can be set off or prolonged by negative life changes and experiences such as acute danger, serious medical illness, the death of a relative or friend, domestic crisis, or unavoidable conflict. Of course, most people who experience stresses like these don't develop agoraphobia. Most likely, the disorder involves a genetic predisposition combined with a host of cultural, familial, and environmental influences.

The frequency and severity of agoraphobic outbreaks vary quite a bit from one person to the next. Some individuals suffer from a general sense of underlying anxiety and have weekly attacks for months at a time. Other people experience milder attacks on a daily basis but then go for months without a major outburst. In a large percentage of the patients who have panic attacks as part of the syndrome, depression accompanies the agoraphobia. Substance-abuse problems can also develop as sufferers try to ease their symptoms by self-medication.

Many people who suffer from agoraphobia become housebound. This man will venture out only in the company of a trusted companion.

HOW TO HELP SOMEONE WHO HAS AN ANXIETY DISORDER

Do:

- Be patient and accepting.
- Act predictably and avoid surprises.
- Ask how you can help.
- Let the person with the disorder set the pace for his or her recovery.
- Find something positive in each small accomplishment.
- Make such statements as

    I know you're in pain, but it's not dangerous.

    Try to breathe slowly.

    You can handle this.

    I'm proud of you.

    It's not this _____ that's bothering you; it's the thought.

Don't:

- Get panicky yourself.
- Make assumptions about what the person needs.
- Settle for the idea that the affected person is permanently disabled.
- Make such statements as

    Just relax.

    Calm down.

    What's the problem?

    Don't be ridiculous.

    Don't be such a coward.

Source: Adapted from suggestions by Dr. Sally Winston, as summarized in Mary Lynn Hendrix, *Understanding Panic Disorder*, NIH Publication No. 95-3509 (Bethesda, Md.: National Institute of Mental Health, 1993).

The difficulty in distinguishing pure agoraphobia from panic disorder, social phobia, and specific phobias has prevented researchers from compiling accurate statistics about the prevalence and long-term prognosis of the disease. Yet, as the *DSM-IV* reports, "anecdotal evidence suggests that some cases may persist for years and be associated with considerable impairment."

THE GENDER QUESTION

Many more women than men suffer from agoraphobia. Some theorists have suggested that this is a result of the expectation in many cultures that women follow the traditional role of remaining at home instead of going out into the world to make a living. According to this line of reasoning, women's "learned helplessness" makes them more likely to develop a fear of public places.

In 1966, when the women's movement was beginning to reexamine issues related to the social position of women, author J. D. W. Andrews noted in her article "Psychotherapy of Phobias" that phobic persons are likely to be dependent on others. Perhaps, Andrews argued, these people were overprotected as children in a manner that was not necessarily affectionate. Five years later, in an article entitled "Phobias After Marriage: A Woman's Declaration of Dependence," author Alexandra Symonds described phobic reactions among women as conflicts between urges toward independence and feelings of dependency. And in 1974, author I. G. Fodor argued in "The Phobic Syndrome in Women" (published in the volume *Women in Therapy*) that "agoraphobia can be considered a caricature of the female role in Western society." Agoraphobia develops, said Fodor, "because the patients in infancy were reinforced for stereotypical female behavior (i.e., helplessness and dependency)."

If women's cultural pattern of dependency helps bring on agoraphobia, a vicious cycle may be at work: the woman's initial dependency may encourage her fear of public places, which in turn may make the woman even more dependent on others to help her cope with matters "out there" in the world.

Yet some researchers have challenged this interpretation of agoraphobia. Perhaps, they say, women are simply more likely than men to report the disorder. In many cultures, after a frightening experience, men are expected to go on with their lives and ignore the trauma. For

Some theorists have proposed that the high proportion of women among agoraphobics can be attributed to the "learned helplessness" created by the tradition in many cultures for women to stay at home instead of going out into the workforce.

women, in contrast, a fearful state is considered more acceptable, making women more likely to admit to problems of a phobic nature.

As with other questions regarding the causes of or the tendency to develop certain illnesses, the true answer is unknown. What is not in dispute, however, is that agoraphobia is a serious problem that demands treatment. Treatment generally follows the same pattern as that described in chapter 2 for the treatment of panic disorder. In the case of extreme agoraphobia, however, some special provisions may be required: it may be necessary, for example, for the therapist to conduct the early sessions in the patient's own home. A combination of medication and psychotherapy is often an effective treatment for patients with this disorder.

Posttraumatic stress disorder (PTSD) can be triggered by a frightening event that the patient has experienced, witnessed, or even simply been told about. Here relatives of crash victims watch as rescue workers remove a body after an American Airlines jet flew into a mountain near Buga, Colombia.

5

POSTTRAUMATIC AND ACUTE STRESS DISORDERS

A s already discussed, any of the disorders examined in this book may be triggered, in part, by a period of stress in the individual's life. Yet two types of anxiety disorders are specifically described as stress disorders: posttraumatic stress disorder and acute stress disorder. Their symptoms are similar, and both occur in the aftermath of what the *DSM-IV* calls "an extremely traumatic event."

POSTTRAUMATIC STRESS DISORDER

Posttraumatic stress disorder (PTSD) is a reaction to a very frightening experience or traumatic event, typically one involving death, serious injury, or grave suffering. Sometimes harm to the individual has actually taken place; in other cases, the mere threat of severe harm may be enough to set off PTSD. The traumatic event may have happened to the patient, or the patient may have witnessed it happening to others. In some cases, the patient has only heard about the event's effect on a family member or close associate, rather than having experienced it or witnessed it firsthand.

Whatever the circumstances of the event itself, PTSD involves the person's reaction of intense horror or fear, often accompanied by a deep sense of helplessness. The disorder can affect people at any age. Characteristically, the patient experiences flashbacks—moments when the awful experience is vividly relived in the mind. According to the NIMH website "Anxiety Disorders," one rape victim described her flashbacks as follows:

> I started having flashbacks. They kind of came over me like a splash of water. I would be terrified. Suddenly I was reliving the rape. Every instant was startling. I felt like my entire head was moving a bit, shaking, but that wasn't so at all. I would get very flushed or a very dry mouth and my breathing changed. I was held in suspension. I wasn't aware of the cushion on the chair that I was sitting in or that my arm was touching a piece of

furniture. . . . Having a flashback can wring you out. You're really shaken.

The precipitating event can be any form of frightening experience: kidnapping, mugging, or other kind of physical attack; automobile, plane, or train crash; or an individual's life-threatening illness. It can be a natural disaster such as a hurricane, earthquake, or flood. Experiences during combat can also trigger the disorder (see the sidebar "The Soldier's Nightmare" on pages 58–59), as can unexpectedly witnessing dead bodies or body parts. Children who have survived abuse or inappropriate sexual contact may also develop PTSD.

SYMPTOMS

Posttraumatic stress disorder is diagnosed only if the symptoms last for more than a month. Sufferers of PTSD are subject to distressing dreams during which the trauma is replayed. Moreover, PTSD sufferers often have flashbacks such as the one described by the rape victim, which may produce a *dissociative state* (a disconnection from reality) lasting seconds, hours, or even days. The individual may experience hallucinations, in which the person sees, hears, or smells things that aren't really there. Even anniversaries of the tragedy or—if it was a natural disaster—weather conditions that resemble those of the day the traumatic event happened may also trigger anxiety.

People with PTSD naturally shun situations that remind them of the fearful incident. They often avoid not only the place where the event occurred but also any objects that were present during the traumatic experience. The avoidance of thoughts connected with the trauma can reach the level of amnesia, in which the person is unable to recall important aspects of the original experience. Sometimes, too, people with PTSD develop a phobia of situations that resemble the trauma or make them recall it.

A type of psychic numbing or emotional anesthesia in the PTSD sufferer usually begins shortly after the catastrophic event occurs. The individual may have diminished interest in pastimes that he or she used to enjoy, including activities associated with tenderness, intimacy, and sexuality. Withdrawal from ordinary activities is not uncommon. Some people feel a sense of foreshortening of the future, believing that they will never have a career, marry, raise children, or have a normal life span. Generally, they display decreased responsiveness to the external world and restricted emotional response. These reactions are part of a psychological attempt by the sufferer to insulate him- or herself from experiencing further pain.

Some researchers have noted that replaying traumatic events through dreams and flashbacks, combined with numbing one's emotions, expresses an all-or-nothing approach to the body's problem of coping with trauma. On one hand, the mind tries to confront stressful events by replaying them again and again, perhaps with the subconscious hope that they will play out differently. On the other hand, the mind blocks out hurt by diminishing feelings. In her book *Trauma and Recovery*, Judith Herman calls this vacillation between two psychic strategies the "dialectic of trauma."

Individuals with posttraumatic stress disorder who made it safely through a harrowing experience when others did not are sometimes plagued by an irrational guilt known as "survivor guilt." Other common symptoms include behaviors of self-destructiveness and impulsiveness;

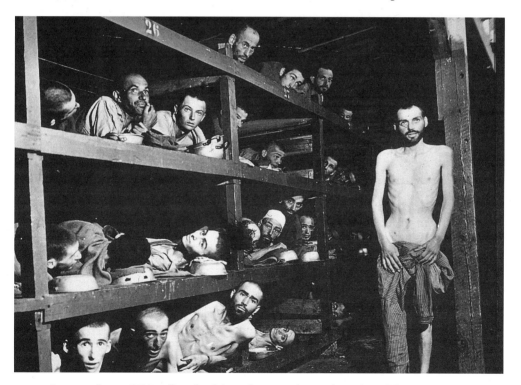

In cases where a PTSD sufferer lived through an experience when others did not, "survivor guilt" may occur. Some concentration camp survivors who watched their families perish in the camps, for example, were plagued by this guilt.

PTSD patients often have flashbacks and dreams that replay the traumatic event. Some suffer from recurring nightmares, which disrupt their sleep.

somatic complaints (physical problems such as headaches, stomach disorders, and backaches); feelings of shame, despair, hopelessness, hostility, and being permanently damaged; and the loss of beliefs that were previously important.

People with PTSD may also show generalized symptoms of anxiety and stress that were not present before the disruptive event occurred. They may have difficulty falling asleep, especially if they are subject to recurrent nightmares. They may seem overly vigilant yet very easily startled. Common behaviors include irritability, outbursts of anger, and trouble concentrating or completing tasks. The anxiety may manifest itself in physical symptoms such as increased heart rate and sweating, blurred vision, dizziness, and breathlessness. The risk of having panic attacks and developing other anxiety disorders increases.

In some cases, delayed onset of PTSD occurs—that is, the symptoms appear six months or more (in some cases, years) after the event. Those who fail to mourn at the time of a loss or are so overcome that they block out all emotions are especially susceptible to experiencing a return of the trauma to haunt them in the future.

WHAT MAKES AN EVENT TRAUMATIC?

Plane crashes, sudden severe illness, and murder are naturally horrifying events. But some of these experiences seem to affect people more deeply than others. What is it about a tragic occurrence that makes it especially likely to cause PTSD?

One factor, of course, is the severity of the event itself. Seeing one's friend murdered is much more disturbing than seeing the same friend held up at gunpoint. Similarly, the individual's proximity to the event is important: being in a plane crash is worse than seeing it at a distance, which in turn is worse than hearing about it secondhand.

An episode of prolonged suffering is often harder to endure than a brief, quick tragedy. A soldier's experience in combat is a good example of many traumatic events spread out over a period of months or years. The soldiers in World War I who experienced shell shock usually did so after prolonged exposure to shelling rather than after the first explosion. Similarly, a prisoner of war, a political prisoner, or a concentration camp inmate typically suffers for extended periods of time in situations of isolation, uncertainty, and the possibility of torture and death. In such cases, the arbitrary nature of the outcome and the victim's inability to change his or her fate make the experience all the more difficult to endure.

The cause of the horrifying experience is another important factor. Tragedies in which human agency is involved—in other words, traumatic events caused by humans rather than by natural forces—are typically more troubling for survivors. In this sense the murder of one person may be harder on the survivor than a hurricane that kills dozens. With little possibility of preventing the tragedy of a hurricane, there is no one to blame, and the survivor's sense of discouragement and hopelessness may be less severe than when coping with human-made disaster.

PREVALENCE

Statistics about the prevalence of PTSD vary widely. Some studies report that about 1 percent of the population has suffered the disorder at one time or another; other studies, however, put the lifetime figure as high as 14 percent. Within any given year, according to NIMH estimates, about 4 percent of the population will experience symptoms of PTSD.

The percentage will be much higher, of course, if the population studied has experienced a recent traumatic event such as war or natural disaster.

Some people may be more susceptible to PTSD than others. For example, previous psychological problems or a family history of anxiety disorders may increase an individual's chance of developing PTSD after he or she experiences a trauma. The *DSM-IV* emphasizes, however, that "this disorder can develop in individuals without any predisposing conditions, particularly if the stressor [the traumatic event] is especially extreme."

ACUTE STRESS DISORDER

Acute stress disorder is very similar to posttraumatic stress disorder, except that in acute stress disorder symptoms appear and are resolved in the four-week period following the traumatic event. Recall that posttraumatic stress disorder refers only to patients whose symptoms persist for longer than a month; acute stress disorder, therefore, is essentially a shorter, quicker version of the illness.

Just about every symptom of posttraumatic stress disorder can also occur in acute stress disorder. However, notes the *DSM-IV*, the patient may also have persistent feelings of derealization (feeling as though what is happening is strange or unreal) and depersonalization (feeling as though the person is detached from him- or herself, observing from outside the body). Frequently, the individual feels guilty being able to get on with his or her normal life, while others have been seriously injured or killed. The acute stress disorder patient may neglect basic health and safety precautions and may even attempt suicide.

Although, compared with other mental illnesses, acute stress disorder is a relatively short-term condition, it is not diagnosed unless the symptoms last for at least two days.

TREATMENT OF STRESS DISORDERS

Treatment for posttraumatic and acute stress disorders often includes a combination of psychotherapy and medication similar to the treatment methods described in previous chapters. However, there are some unique features of treatment that deserve mention.

PSYCHOTHERAPY

In psychotherapy for stress disorders, talking about the hurtful events allows the patient to release pent-up feelings and purge painful emotions by reexperiencing events in a therapeutic context. With the therapist's help, the patient also has the opportunity to gain control over terrifying incidents. Frightening experiences that were fragmentary and unintelligible when they took place may make more sense—and therefore seem more controllable—when the patient reviews them during therapy. Understanding what happened becomes a form of power.

In a cognitive approach, the therapist specifically addresses the patient's anxiety-provoking thoughts. In a behavioral approach, the therapist uses exposure and desensitization techniques to gradually accustom the patient to dealing with places, objects, or situations that he or she has been avoiding. Relaxation and breathing exercises help the patient control the onset of anxiety. Group therapy sessions help the patient release his or her painful emotions, while offering an opportunity for the patient to develop supportive, healing relationships with other people.

In some cases, the patient may benefit from long-term therapy in order to resolve basic psychological conflicts that may be provoking the

In the film Ordinary People, *years after an accident took the life of the oldest son, family members continue to experience the effects. In this scene, the surviving child shares his feelings with a therapist.*

THE SOLDIER'S NIGHTMARE

In the 20th century, as wars became more horrific than ever before, the medical profession had to cope with soldiers who were suffering from long-term psychological disorders that resulted from their wartime experiences.

In World War I, the term *shell shock* was used to describe the symptoms of infantrymen who had been exposed to the relentless artillery explosions of trench warfare. In addition to an extreme sensitivity to loud noises, their symptoms included depression, guilt, nightmares, and flashbacks to scenes of horror.

One of the most notable sufferers of shell shock was Wilfred Owen, a young poet who was hospitalized for the condition in May 1917. In the year after that experience, he wrote the war poems that have earned him lasting fame, describing such grisly scenes as the "twitching agonies" of men caught on barbed wire and the "drowning" of a soldier in a cloud of poison gas. Owen himself was killed in battle just a week before the war's end in November 1918.

PTSD was not uncommon among veterans of the Vietnam War. Here a GI who breaks down after combat is comforted by a fellow soldier.

During World War II the terminology changed: soldiers with similar clusters of symptoms were diagnosed as suffering from *combat fatigue*. Finally, around 1980, after physicians had treated many veterans of the Vietnam War experiencing the same basic symptoms, the term *posttraumatic stress disorder* (PTSD) came into use. Although the majority of Vietnam veterans readjusted to civilian life successfully after the war, in his book *Coping with Trauma* Jon Allen points out that more than a quarter of the troops developed PTSD at one time or another. For many of these veterans the condition became chronic. Over the years, increasing numbers of U.S. war veterans have sought treatment for the disorder.

anxiety. For example, a person whose parent has died in an auto accident may have a complex stress reaction related to problems that he or she had with that parent dating back to childhood. In such cases, in-depth psychotherapy can uncover, and help the patient learn how to deal with, the repressed emotion.

As with any disorder, the earlier an intervention is started, the better. One of the critical messages that must be conveyed to the patient suffering from posttraumatic or acute stress disorder is that now, at last, he or she is safe from harm.

USE OF MEDICATION

Many specific symptoms of stress disorders can be eased by using appropriate medication, which can, in turn, help patients benefit from psychotherapy. Antidepressants, for example, are often useful in treating depressive reactions. Use of benzodiazepines can calm feelings of anxiety and help with difficulty sleeping. These drugs can also help control flashbacks and dissociative reactions. Because benzodiazepines can be addictive, however, extreme caution must be exercised in their use.

A class of drugs known as antipsychotics can also be helpful in treating stress disorders, particularly if hallucinations or other dissociative symptoms have occurred. To prevent these symptoms, a low dose of haloperidol (Haldol) may be prescribed. In addition, clonidine (Catapres) and propranolol (Inderal), which are typically used for high blood pressure, are sometimes prescribed for stress disorders; by blocking physiological arousal, these drugs can reduce some of the symptoms of anxiety.

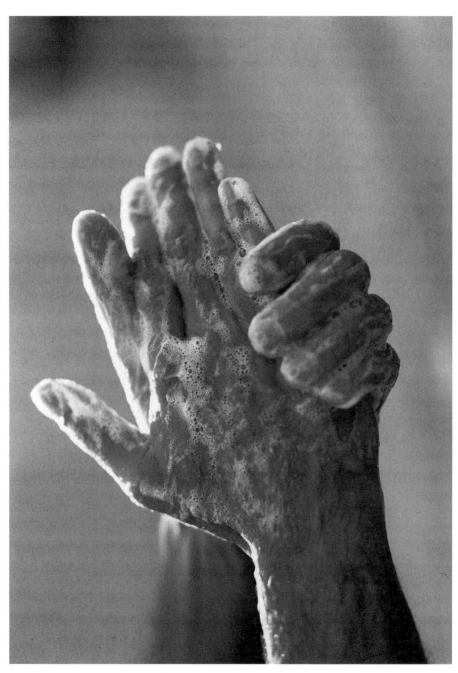

One common form of obsession involves thoughts of contamination. The condition may manifest itself in such behaviors as compulsive hand washing.

6

OBSESSIVE-COMPULSIVE DISORDER

Obsessions are persistent thoughts or ideas that a person cannot avoid, and compulsions are repetitive behaviors that a person feels an irresistible, irrational drive to perform. Obsessive-compulsive disorder can involve either or both of these problems. Often, in fact, an obsession leads to a compulsion.

One common obsession, for example, involves a concern about getting germs on one's hands; this, in turn, may cause the patient to develop a compulsion of repetitive hand washing. Similarly, a persistent doubt about whether one has locked the doors can compel a person to keep checking the doors over and over again.

Although the adult who is practicing irrational rituals generally recognizes their absurdity, this awareness does not relieve him or her of the urge to perform them. An individual who washes his or her hands hundreds of times a day may know perfectly well that those hands are quite clean after a few washings, but stopping the compulsive behavior may still be beyond the person's control. Some patients who suffer from obsessive-compulsive disorder believe that certain aspects of their conduct are reasonable. For instance, a woman who washes her hands until they become raw may admit that such cleanliness is unnecessary when she is in the doctor's office, but she may assert that the precaution is justified when she has been handling money.

The thoughts that plague an obsessive-compulsive do not usually involve such practical problems as financial difficulties, school work, and professional worries. The most common obsessions concern the following:

1. *Thoughts of contamination:* worry about contact with dirt or germs from shaking hands with others, eating, and so on

2. *Repeated doubts:* persistent worry, such as concern that the gas stove was left on, which can lead the sufferer to keep checking the stove repeatedly

3. *A need to have things in a particular order:* a need to place objects in certain ways—for instance, to have all the objects in a room arranged in symmetrical patterns as a way to ward off extreme distress

4. *Aggressive or horrific impulses:* a recurring desire to do something terrible, such as hurt one's child or scream obscenities in church

5. *Intrusive sexual imagery:* thoughts of a pornographic image that repeatedly invades the patient's mind

The most common compulsive behaviors include washing and cleaning, counting, checking, requesting or demanding assurances, repeating actions, and putting things in order. The goal of the compulsion is usually to reduce the person's anxiety or to ward off an assumed terrible occurrence. The compulsions may grow into highly elaborate, idiosyncratic rituals that the patient follows without knowing why he or she does so. For example, an individual tormented by pornographic thoughts may try to block out those images by counting forward and backward to 10, doing so 100 times for each sexually explicit fantasy.

As patients try to resist their obsessions and compulsions, they typically experience mounting tension. And the ritualized thoughts and behaviors themselves commonly take so much time to perform that the patients' overall daily functioning suffers. Imagine how difficult it would be to concentrate on reading a book if you felt compelled to wash your hands every five minutes. Part of the definition of obsessive-compulsive disorder, in fact, is that the unreasonable thoughts or behaviors consume more than an hour of each of the patient's days or cause him or her considerable distress and impairment.

A person with obsessive-compulsive disorder may also develop "secondary" avoidance, as the person tries to stay away from objects or places associated with having to perform elaborate rituals. For instance, a person who is obsessive about dirt may avoid public rest rooms. Another common symptom, hypochondria (believing falsely that one has physical ailments), usually leads the patient to endless visits to physicians in search of reassurance. Feelings of unwarranted guilt, a pathological sense of responsibility, and sleep disturbances are also typical symptoms of people with this disorder.

Obsessive-compulsive disorder can cause many additional problems. In search of relief, the patient may turn to excessive use of alcohol or drugs, including sedatives and tranquilizers. Serious marital, occupational, and social disabilities may result. The disorder is also associated with eating disorders, major depression, phobias, other anxiety disorders, and Tourette's syndrome (usually characterized by facial and vocal tics). Obsessive-compulsive disorder can even leave some patients housebound.

The following case study, related by Dr. Judith L. Rapoport in her book *The Boy Who Couldn't Stop Washing*, indicates how serious, frustrating, and difficult the disease can be.

■   ■   ■

Charles was a 14-year-old boy who spent at least three hours every day in the shower and another two hours getting dressed. He had been following elaborate washing and dressing rituals for a couple of years, and he no longer went to school, because he couldn't get bathed and dressed in time. Psychotherapy and hospitalization hadn't produced any lasting change.

The illness was tearing up Charles's family. His mother knew all the washing was irrational, but she hated to see her son so unhappy, so she helped him scour his room, disinfecting every object with rubbing alcohol. Charles claimed he had to remove a sticky substance from all his surroundings as well as from his body. Because of these extensive cleaning projects, Charles's father avoided coming home in the evenings. Charles had only one friend because the rituals left him little time to leave the house. Other children, even his sisters, teased him about it.

Before the onset of the disease, Charles had been a bright, eager student. He was particularly good in biology, and a teacher had encouraged him to go to college and perhaps become a teacher or doctor. Now such dreams had evaporated.

One day, Charles's mother happened to see a television show about the success Dr. Rapoport was having in treating obsessive-compulsive disorder with medications. After phoning long-distance, she brought her son to Rapoport's office in Bethesda, Maryland, in hopes of finding a cure.

Charles was terrified to have an EEG (electroencephalogram) to test his brain waves, because he feared the sticky substance that would be used to attach the electrodes to his scalp. "Stickiness is terrible. It is some kind of disease; it is like nothing you can understand," Charles told the doctor. Nevertheless, the EEG was done, and Charles stayed up the whole following night trying to wash off the stickiness.

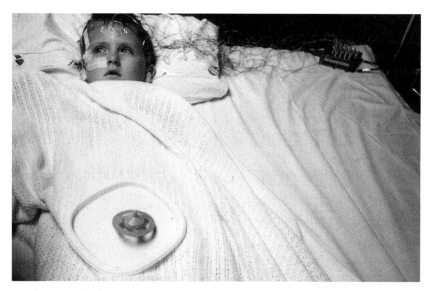

An electroencephalogram (EEG), which tests brain waves, is sometimes used in the diagnosis of obsessive-compulsive disorder. A sticky substance attaches EEG electrodes to this boy's scalp as the test begins.

The worst sticky substance Charles could think of was honey. Touching honey represented extreme danger to him. Yet, within a month, the medication Dr. Rapoport prescribed (a type of antidepressant) had brought the symptoms under control. At this point, Charles took part in an unusual ceremony. He poured honey onto a spoon and grasped the sticky substance in his hand without the slightest concern. For Charles's family, this achievement was tantamount to a miracle.

Charles remained symptom-free for a year. Then he developed some tolerance for the drug, and his symptoms started to return. In such cases, the patient is usually switched to another medication with similar properties. With medication, Charles's rituals were kept at a mild level, and he was able to resume a fairly normal life.

■   ■   ■

As Charles's story indicates, obsessive-compulsive disorder can afflict children and adolescents as well as adults. Unlike most adults, youngsters may not be aware of the irrationality of their ritualized thoughts or behaviors; they may not, in fact, feel distress or think they need to seek help. More often, it is the children's parents who determine that therapeutic help is needed.

THE ILLUSION OF CONTROL

One way of understanding obsessions and compulsions is to see them as the patients' attempts to establish control over themselves and their environment. One person may decide to count to 100 a total of 20 times in an effort to prevent a child from becoming ill—attempting to control the dreaded fate. Another person may avoid stepping on cracks in the sidewalk in a similar effort to ward off disasters. Are these actions illogical? Yes, but symptoms speak with their own peculiar logic. Generally they communicate a sense that too much in life is beyond the person's command.

Although the activities carried out by the obsessive-compulsive patient seem foolish or tedious, a "displacement" has occurred in which the strange behavior substitutes for a larger problem. In reality the person may not be able to control pornographic thoughts, but the ritual of scrubbing his or her face 30 times a day may provide temporary, symbolic relief. Paradoxically, of course, these rituals themselves end up controlling the person who invented them.

PREVALENCE AND COURSE OF THE DISEASE

Obsessive-compulsive disorder occurs at about the same rate among males as among females. Although the disease was once thought to be relatively rare, recent community studies have estimated a lifetime prevalence of 2.5 percent. That is, on average, 2 or 3 out of every 100 people will have the disorder at some time in their lives. Within any given year, about 2 percent of the population suffers from the disease.

Obsessive-compulsive disorder usually develops during adolescence or early adulthood, but it can also start in childhood. Males typically develop the disorder at an earlier age than females. Most males with the disorder display their first symptoms between the ages of 6 and 15; females usually become ill between ages 20 and 29.

The illness usually appears gradually, although rapid onset has been observed in some cases. The majority of people suffering from obsessive-compulsive disorder report that symptoms of the disease wax and wane over the years. The illness typically worsens during times of stress.

SIMILAR DISORDERS

A number of other disorders share some characteristics with obsessive-compulsive disorder, though they differ substantially in important ways.

TWO FAMOUS CASES

S ome very well-known people have suffered from obsessive-compulsive disorder. Samuel Johnson (1709–1784), one of the greatest English literary figures of his age, for example, apparently had a version of the disease. Some of Johnson's various compulsions are recorded in James Boswell's famous *Life of Johnson*.

Johnson would avoid stepping on cracks in paving stones (apropos of the rhyme, "Step on a crack, break your mother's back"). He would touch every post along the street or road where he walked, and if he missed a post, he kept friends waiting while he went back to touch it. Boswell also described the strange way Johnson entered a door:

> He had another peculiarity, of which none of his friends ever ventured to ask an explanation. It appeared to me some superstitious habit, which he had contracted early, and from which he had never called upon his reason to disentangle him. This was his anxious care to go out or in at a door or passage by a certain number of steps from a certain point, or at least so as that either

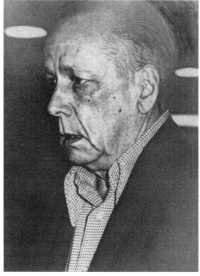

Howard Hughes's obsession with contamination started as mere fastidiousness in childhood. Hughes, shown here both young and old, found it increasingly difficult to keep up with his own eating and grooming rituals.

his right or his left foot (I am not certain which) should constantly make the first actual movement when he came close to the door or passage. Thus I conjecture: for I have, upon innumerable occasions, observed him suddenly stop, and then seem to count his steps with a deep earnestness; and when he had neglected or gone wrong in this sort of magical movement, I have seen him go back again, put himself in a proper posture to begin the ceremony, and, having gone through it, break from his abstraction, walk briskly on, and join his companion.

Johnson's friends and associates saw his behavior as odd rather than sick. The case of American film producer and manufacturer Howard Hughes (1905–76), however, was much more severe. Hughes suffered from an obsessive preoccupation with germs that first manifested itself when he was a child. What began as simple fastidiousness eventually led the reclusive billionaire to seal windows and doors and insulate rooms with layers of paper towels. When his aides brought him documents or food, they had to wear special tissue pads to avoid touching anything with which Hughes came into contact.

Hughes's elaborate eating and toilet rituals took up several hours every day. Ironically, toward the end of his life, he became an unwashed, unkempt figure with matted hair and a straggly beard. When his bathing and cleaning rituals became so overwhelming that he could no longer perform them, he wore only shorts or went unclothed.

Obsessive-compulsive personality disorder, for example, involves a preoccupation with neatness, orderliness, perfection, and control. Despite its name, however, this personality disorder does not involve specific obsessions and compulsions; instead, people with the disorder are overall "control freaks," determined that things be done in exactly the way that they deem correct. (For more on this condition, see the volume *Personality Disorders* in the ENCYCLOPEDIA OF PSYCHOLOGICAL DISORDERS.)

Obsessive-compulsive disorder also differs from the sort of delusional illness in which a person might *believe* that washing his or her hands hundreds of times a day is necessary because extraterrestrial beings require that he or she do so. Charles, the obsessive-compulsive adolescent described earlier in this chapter, was asked if he ever heard voices telling him to wash. He said that he did not.

In the same way, obsessive-compulsive disorder should not be confused with a psychotic disorder. For example, a patient may wash constantly, but in the delusional belief that he is John the Baptist and must prepare for a mass baptism that Jesus has commanded him to perform. Obsessive-compulsives may practice strange behaviors, but they are not delusional or psychotic.

Obsessive-compulsive disorder has also been distinguished from trichotillomania, a condition in which patients compulsively pull out their own hair. The *DSM-IV* categorizes trichotillomania as an impulse-control disorder rather than as an anxiety disorder. Because the two disorders respond to the same medications, however, some researchers consider hair pulling a form of obsessive-compulsive disorder.

GENETIC FACTORS AND TREATMENT

Although no precise cause for obsessive-compulsive disorder has been identified, it, like several other anxiety disorders, appears to have a genetic component. Identical twins are more likely to share the disorder than are fraternal twins. Similarly, a close biological relative of someone who has the disease is more likely than a person from the general population to become obsessive-compulsive. These facts suggest that a genetic predisposition, inherited from one's parents, lays the basis for the disorder. The person's life experiences, however, probably play a part in determining whether the disease actually manifests itself.

Whatever the original cause, the disease's effect on the mind seems to be linked—as with many other psychological conditions—to the actions of *neurotransmitters*, the chemicals that carry messages between nerve cells in the brain. In particular, a neurotransmitter called serotonin appears to play an important part in obsessive-compulsive disorder. Serotonin is closely associated with anger, depression, and impulsiveness. In many obsessive-compulsives, the use of medications that control serotonin have significantly reduced the symptoms of the disease.

By the 1980s, Dr. Rapoport had made some striking breakthroughs in treating the disorder with the drug clomipramine (Anafranil), a potent antidepressant that acts on serotonin. Recently, too, a number of drugs in the class of antidepressants known as SSRIs (selective serotonin reuptake inhibitors) have proved useful, including fluoxetine (Prozac), sertraline (Zoloft), paroxetine (Paxil), and fluvoxamine (Luvox).

What about psychotherapy? The more traditional forms of talk ther-

Behavioral therapy, involving exposure and desensitization, has helped patients learn to stop engaging in their compulsive rituals. Thereafter, relaxation techniques—such as the yoga exercises being performed by this woman—can help decrease the patients' anxiety.

apy have not been very effective in treating obsessive-compulsive disorder; results have been much better with behavioral therapy, especially a type known as exposure and response prevention. In this type of therapy, the first step is similar to the techniques of exposure and desensitization described in previous chapters: that is, with the therapist's support, the patient is first intentionally exposed to a stimulus that triggers the obsessive or compulsive behavior. The second step is to prevent the patient from engaging in the usual compulsive ritual.

If a patient compulsively engages in hand washing because of an obsession with cleanliness, for example, the individual would be asked to dirty his or her hands deliberately. Then the patient would be denied the chance to wash. At first the prevention of hand washing might continue for one or two hours. As the individual's behavioral control increased, the period of response prevention would be extended.

As patients learn to break their compulsive rituals, the relaxation techniques would be used to help them manage their anxiety. Typically, too, behavioral therapy is most effective when combined with the use of medication to help control the symptoms. With this dual approach, many obsessive-compulsives, such as Dr. Rapoport's young patient Charles, are able to subdue or even overcome the disease.

Everyday concerns consume patients who suffer from generalized anxiety disorder. For this man, the constant worry causes headaches, muscle tension, and depression.

7

OTHER ANXIETY DISORDERS

I n addition to the anxiety disorders already described, the *DSM-IV* lists three other kinds: generalized anxiety disorder, anxiety disorder resulting from a general medical condition, and substance-induced anxiety disorder. Let's look at each of these in turn.

GENERALIZED ANXIETY DISORDER

The principal feature of generalized anxiety disorder is excessive, uncontrollable anxiety or worry that focuses on a number of events or activities and that lasts for at least six months. As a result of the constant worry, sufferers of this disorder typically feel restless, tired, or irritable. They may have trouble concentrating and sleeping. They may experience muscle tension, aches and pains, trembling, and shakiness. In short, they often feel keyed up and on edge.

Other physical symptoms may include cold, clammy hands; dry mouth; sweating; nausea or diarrhea; frequent urination; trouble swallowing or the feeling of a lump in the throat; and an exaggerated startle response. Irritable bowel syndrome and headaches frequently accompany this illness, as do other mood or anxiety disorders. Substance abuse and depression are also common.

Although patients do not always identify their worries as excessive, they often report some subjective feeling of distress. Their constant anxiety can also lead to various social, occupational, and family-related problems. As with other anxiety disorders, the *DSM-IV* states that the symptoms must result in "significant distress or impairment" of the patient in order for the disease to be diagnosed.

THE FOCUS OF THE WORRIES

People with generalized anxiety disorder do not suffer from the specific phobias described in chapter 3, such as fear of snakes or insects. They do not worry about being embarrassed in public (as in social phobia) or about having panic attacks (as in panic disorder). What, then, do they worry about?

Adults with generalized anxiety disorder often worry about routine everyday matters, such as job responsibilities, finances, health, household chores, car repairs, or problems with their children or their spouses. They may obsess about being late for appointments. According to the NIMH website entitled "Anxiety Disorders," one sufferer of this disorder reported, "I'd worry about what I was going to fix for a dinner party, or what would be a great present for somebody. . . . My heart would race or pound. And that would make me worry more." A person with generalized anxiety disorder often shifts from one worrisome topic to another.

Children and adolescents with this disorder tend to obsess about their competence or performance at school or at sports. They may become perfectionists, continuously redoing tasks to correct minor flaws. They may be overzealous in seeking approval and require tremendous reassurance from others. Some young people may even focus on world catastrophes, such as earthquakes and nuclear war, suffering a truly generalized anxiety about matters that they cannot possibly influence.

PREVALENCE, COURSE, AND TREATMENT

The *DSM-IV* reports a lifetime prevalence of 5 percent for generalized anxiety disorder; that is, about 5 in every 100 people will experience the disease at some time in their lives. The NIMH estimates that 3 to 4 percent of the population suffers from the disease each year. The disorder is slightly more common among women than among men.

Many individuals with generalized anxiety disorder claim that it has plagued them all their lives. More than half report that the disorder started during childhood or adolescence, although onset after age 20 is not uncommon. In many cases, the symptoms decrease as a person ages. The disease is chronic, but it fluctuates in response to stress. At times when life becomes stressful, the disorder is most likely to strike.

Treatment usually involves cognitive-behavioral therapy and relaxation techniques. Patients who experience muscle aches and tension may also benefit from biofeedback exercises, in which they can learn to gain some voluntary control over their physical responses. Research into the benefits of medication is not yet conclusive. The NIMH and other agencies report that use of the drug buspirone (BuSpar) has proven helpful in a number of cases. Benzodiazepines, such as alprazolam (Xanax) and lorazepam (Ativan), are also sometimes prescribed.

Generalized anxiety disorder usually increases in severity during times of stress. Cognitive-behavioral therapy has helped this woman control the disorder.

ANXIETY DISORDER RESULTING FROM A GENERAL MEDICAL CONDITION

Anxiety disorder resulting from a general medical condition refers to a clinically significant form of anxiety determined to be the direct, physiological result of another medical problem. The symptoms vary from generalized anxiety to obsessive behavior, compulsive behavior, and panic attacks.

The following lists just a few of the many illnesses that have been known to cause an anxiety disorder:

- Arrhythmia (erratic beating of the heart)
- Congestive heart failure

- Hyper- and hypothyroidism (too much or too little activity of the thyroid gland)
- Hypoglycemia (low blood sugar)
- Infectious diseases
- Metabolic disorders
- Neurological conditions
- Pneumonia
- Respiratory problems
- Vitamin deficiencies

Particularly when chronic worrying begins at a relatively late stage in life and when there is no family history of the disorder, a thorough physical examination is recommended to determine whether a medical condition is the source of an anxiety disorder.

SUBSTANCE-INDUCED ANXIETY DISORDER

Anxiety disorders can also be caused by various substances, including medications, alcohol, illegal drugs, and toxins. (See the sidebar for a list of common substances.) Depending on the nature of the substance, anxiety may result from intoxication during use of the substance or from withdrawal following use. Symptoms include panic attacks, phobias, obsessive and compulsive behavior, and generalized anxiety.

The diagnosis of substance-induced anxiety disorder is not applied to occasional problems caused by drugs or alcohol, but rather to instances in which the anxiety reaction produces significant distress or impairment. People with this condition may be incapable of functioning normally in social situations or at work. Symptoms may also include loss of balance or consciousness, bladder or bowel problems, slurred speech, headaches, and partial amnesia (loss of memory). Some substances, such as benzodiazepines, are associated with a protracted withdrawal process in which symptoms may not develop for as long as four weeks after use of the substance has ceased.

In an age when pharmaceutical products of all sorts are a common part of daily life, substance abuse has become an overwhelming problem. Anxiety disorders are just one of the many mental illnesses that drug use can trigger. It is crucial for a patient suffering from severe anx-

Alcohol is one of the many substances that can trigger anxiety disorders. A person who experiences serious symptoms should inform his or her physician of any past or present substance abuse.

SOME SUBSTANCES THAT MAY CAUSE AN ANXIETY REACTION

Medications, illegal drugs, and toxins have been identified as anxiety-inducing substances. Marijuana and cocaine, shown here, are counted among the offending drugs.

T he list of substances that may cause substance-induced anxiety disorder is virtually endless. The anxiety reaction can be especially severe when the substance has been abused by a person particularly susceptible to developing the disorder. Here are just a few of the kinds of substances that can trigger this type of problem:

Alcohol	Anesthetics
Amphetamines	Anticonvulsants
Analgesics (painkillers)	Antidepressants

Antihistamines
Antiparkinsonian medications
Antipsychotic drugs
Caffeine
Cannabis (marijuana)
Carbon monoxide
Cardiovascular medicines
Cocaine (and crack)
Contraceptives (the oral varieties)
Corticosteroids
Gasoline
Hallucinogens (such as LSD and
   PCP)

Heroin
Hypnotics (sleeping pills)
Inhalants (glue, nail-polish
   remover, nitrous oxide, and
   other substances abused
   through inhalation)
Insecticides
Insulin
Lithium carbonate
Nerve gases
Paint
Sedatives
Thyroid preparations

Some of these substances, such as insulin and antidepressants, are vital medications to people suffering from diabetes or depression. Others, such as caffeine and paint, are not problematic under ordinary circumstances. The key, in most cases, is how the substance is used. Normal, careful, medically approved use seldom causes an anxiety disorder.

iety symptoms to report any history of substance abuse to his or her doctor. Treatment can take various forms, including medication for the immediate anxiety symptoms and psychotherapy to help the patient avoid substance abuse in the future.

Although there is overlap among the symptoms for generalized anxiety disorder, anxiety disorder resulting from a general medical condition, and substance-abuse anxiety disorder, health care professionals can successfully diagnose individuals who have these illnesses. With a clear diagnosis, a patient can then receive the treatment or treatments appropriate for his or her disorder.

APPENDIX

FOR MORE INFORMATION

American Academy of Child and Adolescent Psychiatry (AACAP)
3615 Wisconsin Avenue, NW
Washington, DC 20016-3007
(202) 966-7300
http://www.aacap.org/

American Psychiatric Association (APA)
1400 K Street, NW
Washington, DC 20005
(202) 682-6000
http://www.psych.org/

Anxiety Disorders Association of America (ADAA)
11900 Parklawn Drive, Suite 100
Rockville, MD 20852-2624
(301) 231-9350
http://www.adaa.org/

Canadian Mental Health Association (CMHA)
2160 Yonge Street, 3rd Floor
Toronto, Ontario M4S 2Z3
Canada
(416) 484-7750
http://www.cmha.ca/

National Alliance for the Mentally Ill (NAMI)
200 North Glebe Road, Suite 1015
Arlington, VA 22203-3754
(703) 524-7600
(800) 950-6264
http://www.nami.org/

National Institute of Mental Health (NIMH)
NIMH Public Inquiries
6001 Executive Boulevard, Room 8184 MSC 9663
Bethesda, MD 20892-9663
(301) 443-4513
E-mail: nimhinfo@nih.gov
http://www.nimh.nih.gov/

National Mental Health Association (NMHA)
1021 Prince Street
Alexandria, VA 22314-2971
(800) 969-6642
http://www.nmha.org/

APPENDIX

BIBLIOGRAPHY

Allen, Jon G. *Coping with Trauma: A Guide to Self-Understanding.* Washington, D.C.: American Psychiatric Press, 1995.

American Psychiatric Association. *Diagnostic and Statistical Manual of Mental Disorders,* 4th ed. Washington, D.C.: American Psychiatric Association, 1994.

Andrews, J. D. W. "Psychotherapy of Phobias," *Psychological Bulletin* 66 (1966): 455–80.

"Anxiety Disorders." National Institute of Mental Health, Bethesda, Maryland [on-line]. Accessed September 1999. Available at http://www.nimh.nih.gov/anxiety/.

Barlow, David H. *Anxiety and Its Disorders: The Nature and Treatment of Anxiety and Panic.* New York: Guilford Press, 1988.

Boulenger, J. P., T. W. Unde, E. A. Wolff, et al. "Increased Sensitivity to Caffeine in Patients with Panic Disorder: Preliminary Evidence," *Archives of General Psychiatry* 41 (1984): 1067–71.

Boyd, J. H. "Use of Mental Health Services for the Treatment of Panic Disorder," *American Journal of Psychiatry* 36 (1986): 1569–74.

Charney, D. S., G. R. Heninger, and A. Breier. "A Noradrenergic Function in Panic Anxiety," *Archives of General Psychiatry* 41 (1984): 751–63.

Clevenger, S. W. "Heart Disease in Insanity and a Case of Panphobia," *Alien Neurolo* 7 (1890): 535–43.

Coryell, W., R. Noyes, and J. Clancy. "Excess Mortality in Panic Disorder: A Comparison with Primary Unipolar Depression," *Archives of General Psychiatry* 39 (1982): 701–3.

Coryell, W., R. Noyes, and J. D. House. "Mortality Among Outpatients with Anxiety Disorders," *American Journal of Psychiatry* 143 (1986): 508–10.

Darwin, Charles. *The Expression of the Emotions in Man and Animals.* 1872. Reprint (3rd ed.). Edited by Paul Ekman. Oxford, England: Oxford University Press, 1998.

Denny, M. Ray, ed. *Fear, Avoidance, and Phobias: A Fundamental Analysis.* Hillsdale, N.J.: Lawrence Erlbaum Associates, 1991.

Fodor, I. G. "The Phobic Syndrome in Women." In *Women in Therapy,* ed. V. Franks and V. Burtle. New York: Brunner/Mazel, 1974.

Freud, Sigmund. *A General Introduction to Psychoanalysis.* New York: Simon and Schuster, 1971.

Gelinas, D. J. *Treatment of Adult Survivors of Incest.* Washington, D.C.: American Psychiatric Press, 1993.

Hendrix, Mary Lynn. *Understanding Panic Disorder.* NIH Publication No. 95-3509. Bethesda, Md.: National Institute of Mental Health, 1993.

Herman, Judith. *Trauma and Recovery.* New York: Basic Books, 1992.

Kierkegaard, Søren. *The Concept of Dread,* trans. Walter Lowrie. Princeton, N.J.: Princeton University Press, 1957.

Marks, Isaac M. *Fears, Phobias, and Ritual: Panic, Anxiety, and Their Disorders.* New York: Oxford University Press, 1987.

Marshall, J. R. "Are Many Irritable Bowel Syndromes Actually Panic Disorder?" *Postgraduate Medicine* 83 (1988): 206–9.

May, Rollo. *The Meaning of Anxiety.* New York: Ronald Press, 1950.

McCann, I. Lisa, and Laurie Ann Pearlman. *Psychological Trauma and the Adult Survivor: Theory, Therapy, and Transformation.* New York: Brunner/Mazel, 1990.

Michelson, Larry, and L. Michael Ascher. *Anxiety and Stress Disorders: Cognitive-Behavioral Assessment and Treatment.* New York: Guilford Press, 1987.

Panic Disorder Treatment and Referral: Information for Health Care Professionals. NIH Publication No. 94-3642. Bethesda, Md.: National Institute of Mental Health, 1994. Available at http://www.nimh.nih.gov/anxiety/.

Rapoport, Judith L. *The Boy Who Couldn't Stop Washing: The Experience and Treatment of Obsessive-Compulsive Disorder.* New York: E. P. Dutton, 1989.

Roth, M., R. Noyes, and G. Burrows, eds. *Handbook of Anxiety.* Amsterdam: Elsevier, 1992.

Scruton, David L., ed. *Sociophobics: The Anthropology of Fear.* Boulder, Colo.: Westview Press, 1986.

Symonds, Alexandra. "Phobias After Marriage: A Woman's Declaration of Dependence," *American Journal of Psychoanalysis* 31 (1971): 144–52.

Zal, Michael H. *Panic Disorder: The Great Pretender.* New York: Insight Books, 1990.

APPENDIX

FURTHER READING

Allen, Jon G. *Coping with Trauma: A Guide to Self-Understanding.* Washington, D.C.: American Psychiatric Press, 1995.

American Psychiatric Association. *Diagnostic and Statistical Manual of Mental Disorders.* 4th ed. Washington, D.C.: American Psychiatric Press, 1994.

"Anxiety Disorders." National Institute of Mental Health, Bethesda, Maryland [on-line]. Available at http://www.nimh.nih.gov/anxiety/.

Beck, Aaron T., Gary Emery, and Ruth L. Greenberg. *Anxiety Disorders and Phobias: A Cognitive Perspective.* New York: Basic Books, 1990.

Carmin, Cheryl N., C. Alec Pollard, Teresa Flynn, and Barbara G. Markway. *Dying of Embarrassment: Help for Social Anxiety and Phobia.* Oakland, Calif.: New Harbinger, 1992.

Carter, Rosalynn, with Susan K. Golant. *Helping Someone with Mental Illness.* New York: Times Books, 1999.

Herman, Judith. *Trauma and Recovery.* New York: Basic Books, 1992.

Rapoport, Judith L. *The Boy Who Couldn't Stop Washing: The Experience and Treatment of Obsessive-Compulsive Disorder.* New York: E. P. Dutton, 1989.

Schneier, Franklin, and Lawrence A. Welkowitz. *The Hidden Face of Shyness: Understanding and Overcoming Social Anxiety.* New York: Avon, 1996.

Wilson, R. Reid. *Don't Panic: Taking Control of Anxiety Attacks.* New York: HarperCollins, 1996.

Zal, Michael H. *Panic Disorder: The Great Pretender.* New York: Insight Books, 1990.

APPENDIX

GLOSSARY

Acute stress disorder: fear, anxiety, and other symptoms resulting from a traumatic experience; similar to, but not as long lasting as, posttraumatic stress disorder.

Agoraphobia: a severe anxiety about being in open areas or public places, which is frequently considered a symptom of panic disorder.

Antidepressants: a group of medications, of several different chemical types, often used for treating depression; some drugs in this category are also effective for such anxiety-related conditions as panic attacks and obsessive-compulsive disorder.

Anxiety disorder resulting from a general medical condition: excessive anxiety resulting from another medical condition.

Benzodiazepines: a class of drugs, often known as "major tranquilizers," sometimes prescribed for anxiety conditions and other psychological disorders.

Cognitive-behavioral therapy: a type of psychotherapy (talk therapy) that focuses on changing specific thought patterns (cognitions) and behaviors that contribute to a patient's psychological disorder; cognitive-behavioral therapy generally involves a narrower focus and a shorter time span than older forms of psychotherapy.

Dissociative state: a feeling of being disconnected from reality.

Exposure technique: a behavioral therapy approach consisting of deliberate exposure to an anxiety-producing stimulus in order to help the patient learn to control his or her reaction; sometimes the technique includes response prevention, in which the patient is actually prevented from reacting in the usual way.

Fight-or-flight response: a set of changes in the body including increased heart and respiratory rates, brought about by the release of the hormones adrenaline and noradrenaline in response to extreme danger.

Generalized anxiety disorder: excessive, uncontrollable anxiety or worry that focuses on a number of events or activities, lasts for at least six months, and cannot be ascribed to another anxiety disorder.

Hyperventilation: an abnormally fast or deep breathing pattern that can make a person dizzy; a common feature of panic attacks.

Neurotransmitters: chemical substances, such as serotonin, that convey impulses between nerves.

Obsessive-compulsive disorder: recurrent obsessions (persistent thoughts or ideas) or compulsions (repetitive, ritualistic behaviors) that are time-consuming or distressful, significantly impairing a person's life.

Panic attack: intense fear or discomfort that begins suddenly, builds quickly to a peak, and is accompanied by such symptoms as trembling, heart palpitations, dizziness, sweating, shortness of breath, and a feeling of being smothered.

Panic disorder: recurrent, unexpected panic attacks accompanied by worry about future attacks or by other behavioral changes.

Phobia: persistent, irrational fear of an object, activity, or situation; major subtypes include specific phobia (fear of a particular object or specific situation) and social phobia (persistent fear of socially embarrassing situations).

Posttraumatic stress disorder: fear, horror, and other symptoms resulting from a traumatic experience, such as child abuse or war.

Substance-induced anxiety disorder: prominent anxiety symptoms directly related to a person's exposure to a particular substance, such as a drug or a poison.

Systematic desensitization: a variety of exposure techniques in which the patient gradually undergoes increased exposure to an anxiety-producing stimulus in order to decrease his or her sensitivity to the stimulus over time.

APPENDIX

INDEX

APPENDIX

PICTURE CREDITS

page

Senior Consulting Editor Carol C. Nadelson, M.D., is president and chief executive officer of the American Psychiatric Press, Inc., staff physician at Cambridge Hospital, and Clinical Professor of Psychiatry at Harvard Medical School. In addition to her work with the American Psychiatric Association, which she served as vice president in 1981–83 and president in 1985–86, Dr. Nadelson has been actively involved in other major psychiatric organizations, including the Group for the Advancement of Psychiatry, the American College of Psychiatrists, the Association for Academic Psychiatry, the American Association of Directors of Psychiatric Residency Training Programs, the American Psychosomatic Society, and the American College of Mental Health Administrators. In addition, she has been a consultant to the Psychiatric Education Branch of the National Institute of Mental Health and has served on the editorial boards of several journals. Doctor Nadelson has received many awards, including the Gold Medal Award for significant and ongoing contributions in the field of psychiatry, the Elizabeth Blackwell Award for contributions to the causes of women in medicine, and the Distinguished Service Award from the American College of Psychiatrists for outstanding achievements and leadership in the field of psychiatry.

Consulting Editor Claire E. Reinburg, M.A., is editorial director of the American Psychiatric Press, Inc., which publishes about 60 new books and six journals a year. She is a graduate of Georgetown University in Washington, D.C., where she earned bachelor of arts and master of arts degrees in English. She is a member of the Council of Biology Editors, the Women's National Book Association, the Society for Scholarly Publishing, and Washington Book Publishers.

Linda Bayer, Ph.D., graduated from Boston University and received a master's degree in English and a doctorate in humanities from Clark University. She worked with patients suffering from substance abuse and other problems at a guidance center and in the Boston public school system. Bayer was also a high school teacher be-fore joining the faculties of several universities, including Wesleyan University, Hartford College for Women, American University, Boston University, and the U.S. Naval Academy. At the Hebrew University in Israel, she occupied the Sam and Ayala Zacks Chair. Bayer has also worked as a newspaper editor and a syndicated columnist, winning a Simon Rockower Award for excellence in journalism. Her published works include *The Gothic Imagination, The Blessing and the Curse* (a novel), and several books on substance abuse, as well as five volumes in the ENCYCLOPEDIA OF PSYCHOLOGICAL DISORDERS. Bayer is currently a senior speechwriter and a strategic analyst at the White House. She is the mother of two children, Lev and Ilana.